W9-ARH-282

Mapping the Continents

Mapping Europe

Paul Rockett

with artwork by Mark Ruffle

Crabtree Publishing Company
www.crabtreebooks.com

Crabtree Publishing Company
www.crabtreebooks.com
1-800-387-7650

Published in Canada
616 Welland Ave.
St. Catharines, ON
L2M 5V6

Published in the United States
PMB 59051, 350 Fifth Ave.
59th Floor,
New York, NY

Published in 2017 by CRABTREE PUBLISHING COMPANY.

First published in 2015 by The Watts Publishing Group
(An imprint of Hachette Children's Group)

Author: Paul Rockett

Editorial director: Kathy Middleton

Editors: Adrian Cole, and Ellen Rodger

Proofreader: Wendy Scavuzzo

Series design and illustration:
Mark Ruffle, www.rufflebrothers.com

Prepress technician: Katherine Berti

Print and production coordinator: Katherine Berti

Printed in Canada/072016/PB20160525

Picture credits:
Ace Stock/Alamy: 25br; Dcoetzee/CC , Wikimedia: 26bl; A Howden International/Alamy: 25bl; Pavel Konovalov/ Dreamstime: 19bl; Lukiyanova Natalia/frenta/Shutterstock: 19br; Supergenijalac/Dreamstime: 21tc; CC Wikimedia: 4c, 6-7; Rob Wilson/Shutterstock: 21tr.

Library and Archives Canada Cataloguing in Publication

Rockett, Paul, author
Mapping Europe / Paul Rockett.

(Mapping the continents)
Includes index.
Issued in print and electronic formats.
ISBN 978-0-7787-2615-9 (hardback).--
ISBN 978-0-7787-2621-0 (paperback).--
ISBN 978-1-4271-1782-3 (html)

1. Europe--Juvenile literature. 2. Cartography--Europe--Juvenile literature. 3. Europe--Geography--Juvenile literature. 4. Europe--Description and travel--Juvenile literature. 5. Europe--Maps--Juvenile literature. I. Title.

D2020.R64 2016 j914 C2016-902656-6
C2016-902657-4

Library of Congress Cataloging-in-Publication Data

Names: Rockett, Paul, author.
Title: Mapping Europe / Paul Rockett.
Description: New York, New York : Crabtree Publishing Co., 2017. |
Series: Mapping the continents | Includes index. |
Identifiers: LCCN 2016016675 (print) | LCCN 2016024422 (ebook) |
ISBN 9780778726159 (reinforced library binding) |
ISBN 9780778726210 (pbk.) |
ISBN 9781427117823 (electronic HTML)
Subjects: LCSH: Europe--Juvenile literature. | Cartography--Europe--Juvenile literature. | Europe--Geography--Juvenile literature. | Europe--Description and travel--Juvenile literature.
Classification: LCC D1051 .R64 2017 (print) | LCC D1051 (ebook) |
DDC 915--dc23
LC record available at https://lccn.loc.gov/2016016675

Contents

Where is Europe?

Europe is part of a giant landmass that borders Asia, and includes a small number of islands in surrounding seas and oceans. Many early maps were made by European explorers who traveled beyond the continent, discovering new lands.

What does a map do?

Maps show you where things are and can be used to help you get from one place to another. They can also show you the distance between two places, but the map needs to be accurate and to scale.

European map-making

This is one of the first maps of the world. It was created in 1482 in Germany, following instructions that were originally written in 150 A.C.E. by a Greek **astronomer**, Ptolemy.

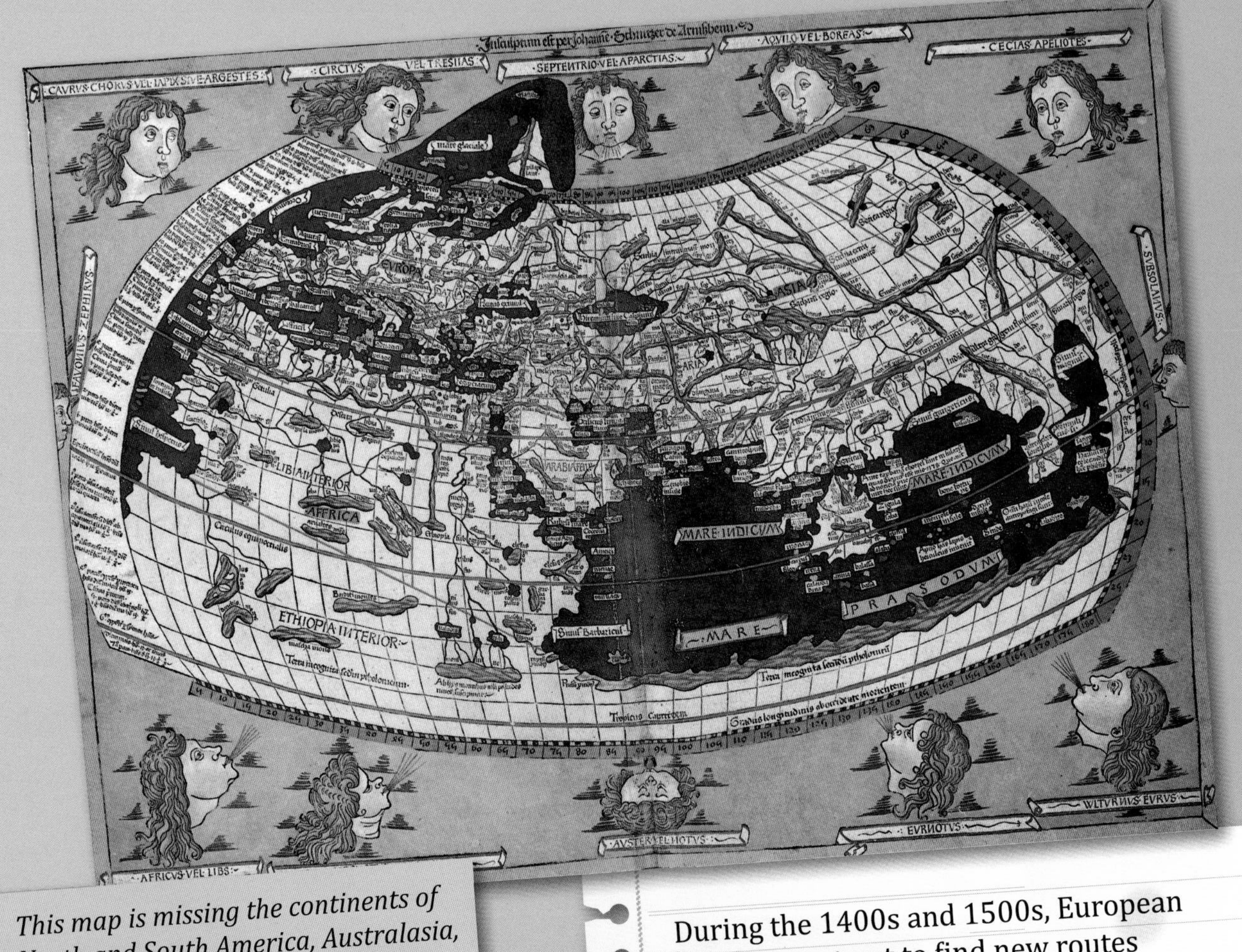

This map is missing the continents of North and South America, Australasia, and Antarctica. Those places had not yet been visited by Europeans.

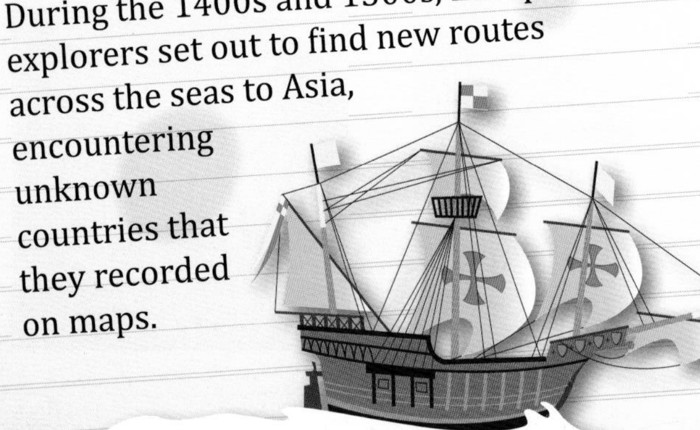

During the 1400s and 1500s, European explorers set out to find new routes across the seas to Asia, encountering unknown countries that they recorded on maps.

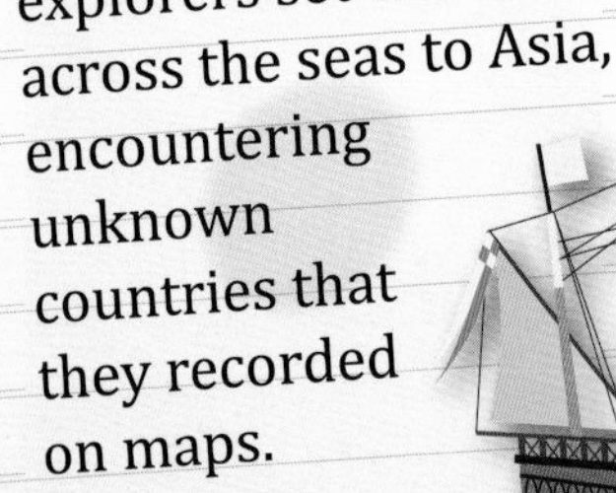

Latitude and longitude

World maps feature a grid of imaginary lines called **latitude** and **longitude**. These lines are numbered so that places can be located using the number of the latitude line first, followed by the number of the longitude line.

*Lines of latitude go round the world from east to west. The **equator** is a line of latitude (0°).*

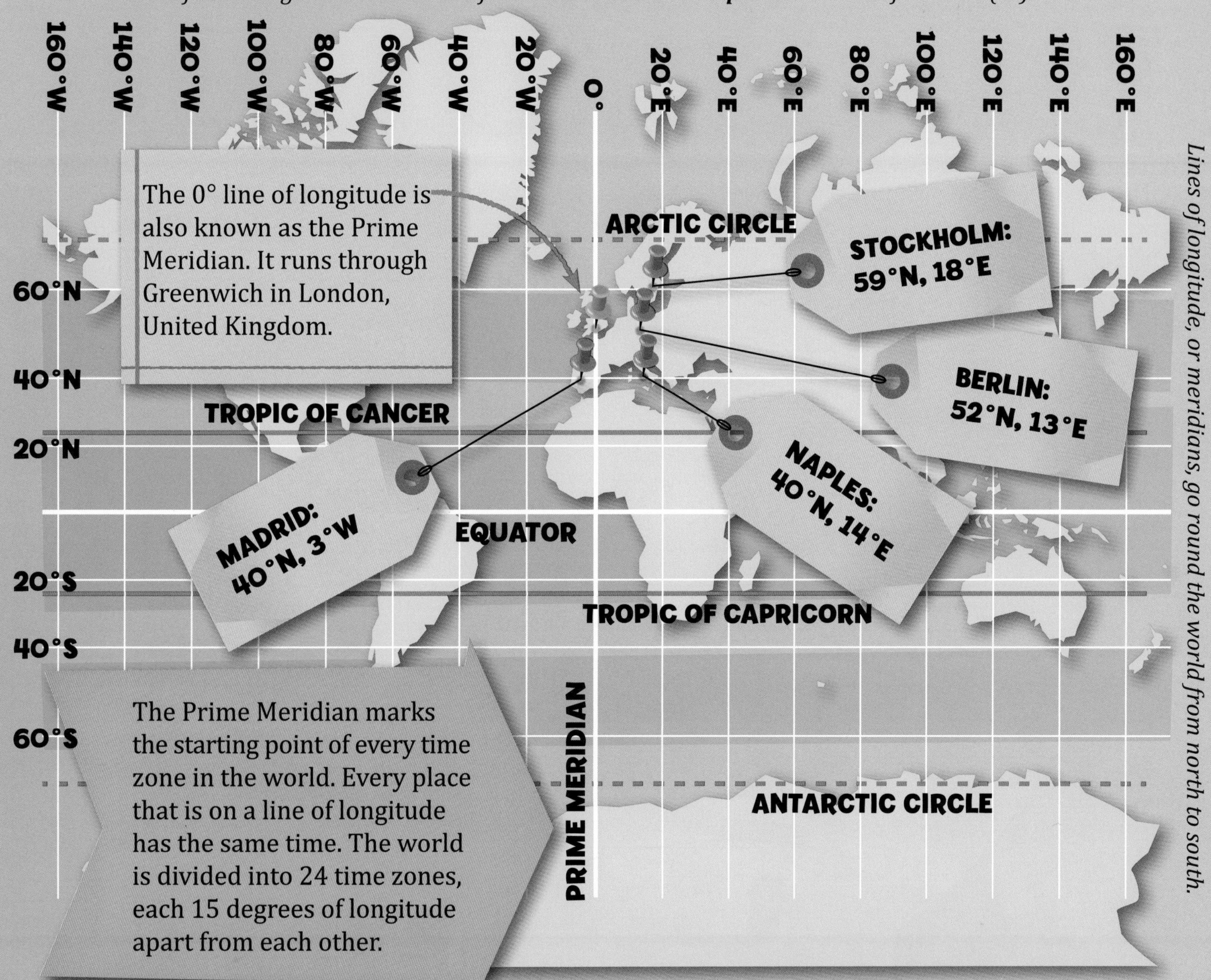

Lines of longitude, or meridians, go round the world from north to south.

What surrounds Europe?

You can use a map to locate a place by using grid references, such as lines of latitude and longitude. You can also describe a place in relation to the compass points of north, east, south, or west.

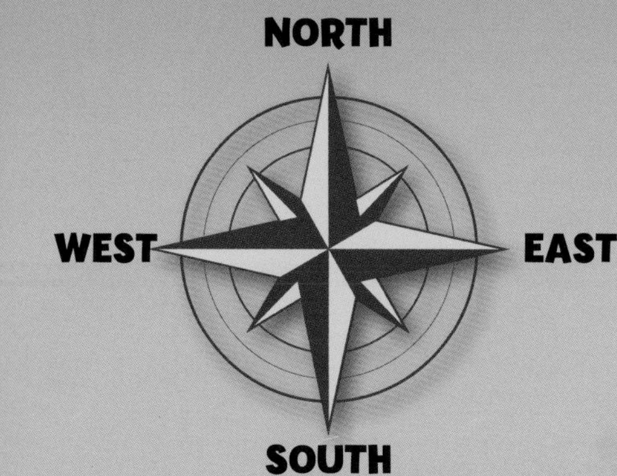

Europe is south of the Arctic Ocean

Europe is east of the Atlantic Ocean

Europe is west of Asia

Europe is north of the Mediterranean Sea

Europe is north of Africa

Countries

Europe may be the second smallest continent, but it has the third-largest population of around 742.5 million people.

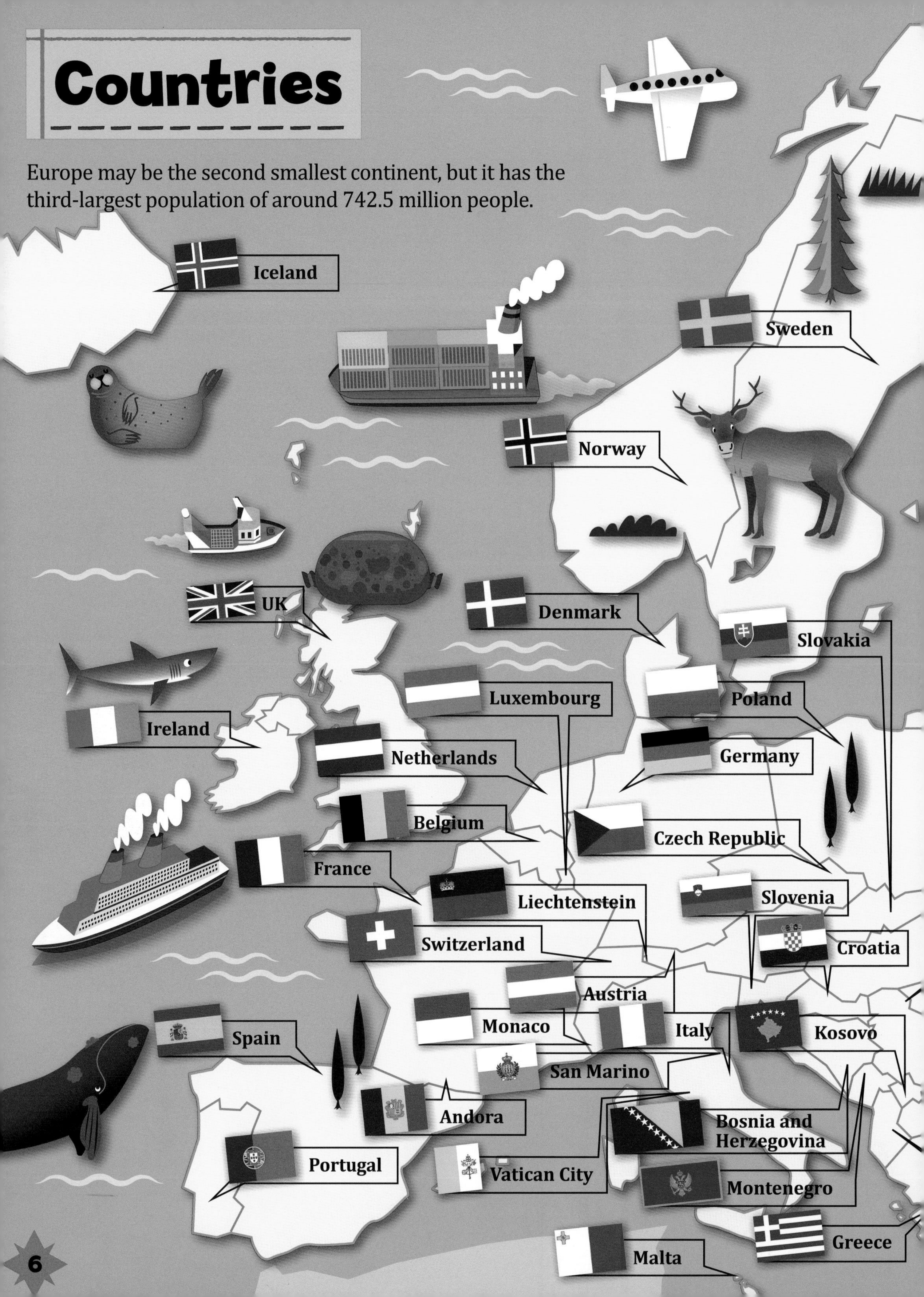

Transcontinental countries

There are five countries in Europe that also cross over into the continent of Asia. They are Russia, Azerbaijan, Georgia, Kazakhstan, and Turkey. These are called **transcontinental** countries.

Dividing and uniting Europe

The Europe we know today is different from the Europe that existed 25 years ago, and even more unrecognizable from that of 10,000 years ago. The number of countries and their borders have changed throughout history.

20th century Europe

During the 1900s, the map of Europe, particularly in the East, went through many changes.

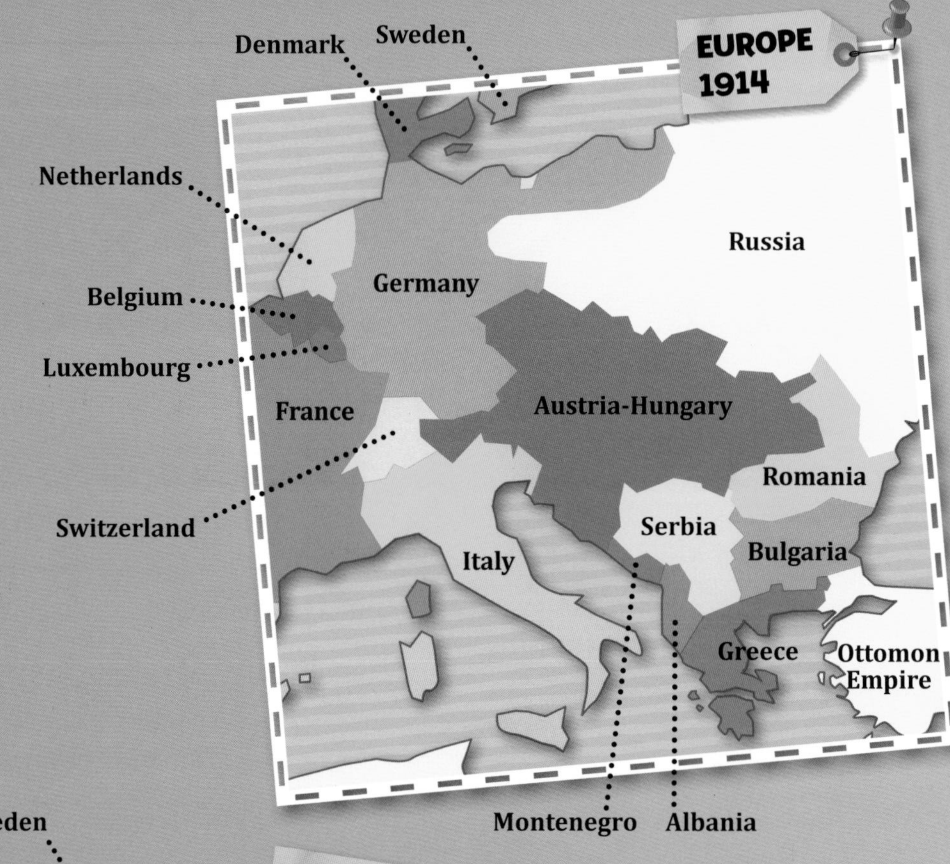

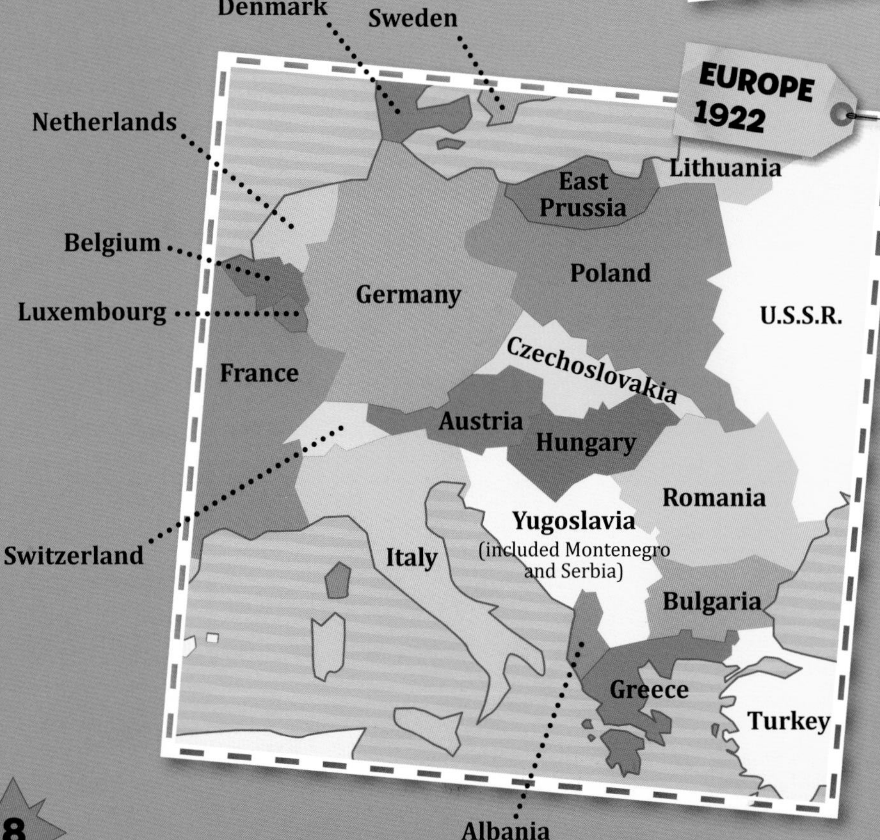

After the First World War (1914–1918), the borders within Europe were redrawn, changing the centers of power. This created many new countries. Some countries lost land, others gained land, and a few such as the Ottoman Empire and Austria-Hungary completely disappeared.

After the Second World War (1939–1945), Germany was divided into two countries: East Germany and West Germany. In 1961, a wall was built splitting the capital city, Berlin, in two. One half belonged to **communist** East Germany, and the other half to **democratic** West Germany.

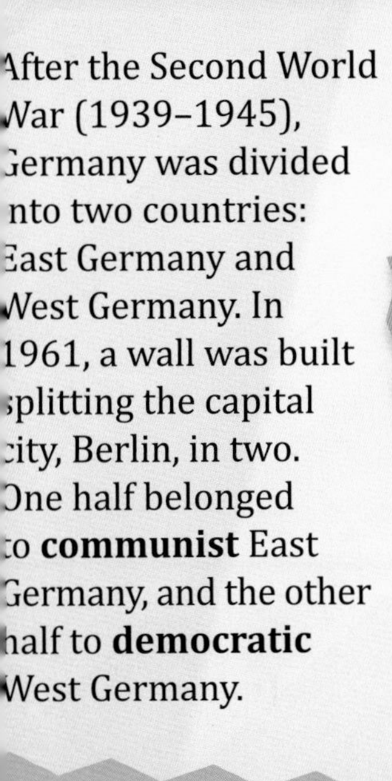

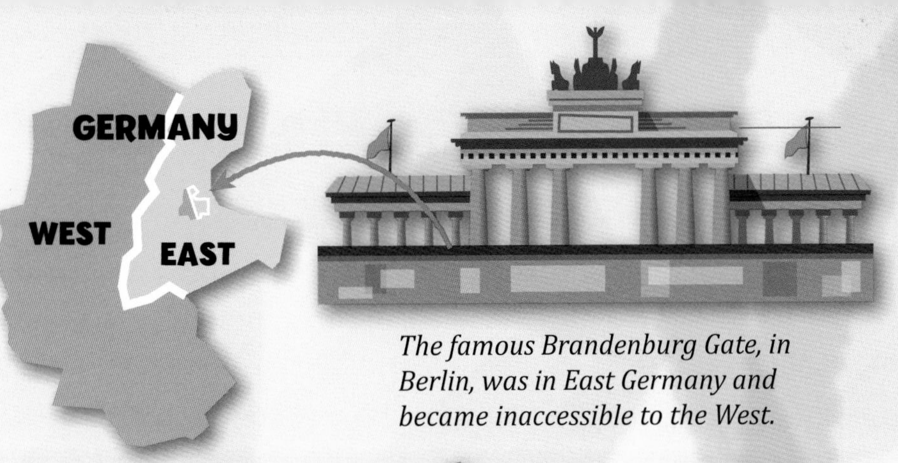

The famous Brandenburg Gate, in Berlin, was in East Germany and became inaccessible to the West.

In 1989, the Berlin Wall came down, and not long after, East and West Germany were reunited as one country. This moment led to a gradual change of politics in Eastern Europe.

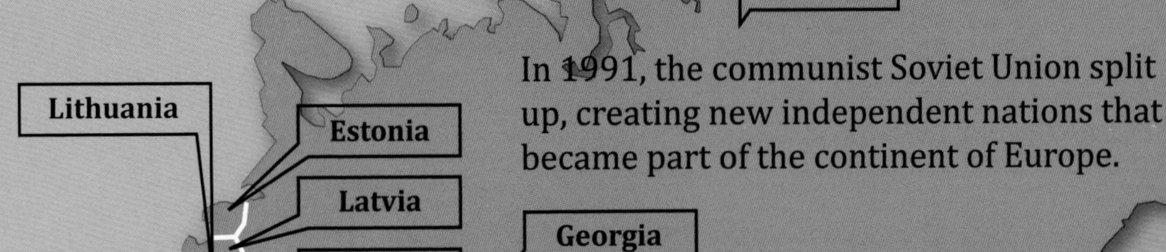

In 1991, the communist Soviet Union split up, creating new independent nations that became part of the continent of Europe.

The European Union

Although each country within Europe has its own government and parliament, some work together as part of a group called the European Union (EU). The member states of the EU help each other with political and economic problems.

At first, there were just six countries in the European Economic Community. There are now 28 countries, known as member states. Nineteen of these countries share the same **currency**, the Euro.

The EU is made up of the following countries:

Year they joined the EU	Countries					
1958	Belgium	France	Germany	Italy	Luxembourg	Netherlands
1973	Denmark	Ireland	United Kingdom			
1981	Greece					
1986	Portugal	Spain				
1995	Austria	Finland	Sweden			
2004	Cyprus	Czech Republic	Estonia	Hungary	Latvia	Lithuania
	Poland	Slovakia	Malta	Slovenia		
2007	Bulgaria	Romania				
2013	Croatia					

Regions of Europe

When people talk about Europe, they often divide it into regions. The regions are connected by their location and often share a similar history and language. The four main points of the compass are used to split Europe into four regions: northern Europe, eastern Europe, southern Europe, and western Europe.

Northern Europe

Northern Europe is made up of the following countries: Iceland, Norway, Sweden, Finland, Denmark, the United Kingdom, Ireland, Estonia, Latvia, and Lithuania.

British Isles

"The British Isles" refers to a collection of islands. It includes the United Kingdom and Ireland, and although it has the word "British" in its title, it does not describe one group of people or nationality.

The United Kingdom is made up of Northern Ireland, Scotland, Wales, and England. "Great Britain" refers to just Scotland, Wales, and England.

Western Europe

The countries of western Europe are: France, Germany, Austria, Belgium, Liechtenstein, Monaco, Netherlands, Luxembourg, and Switzerland.

Southern Europe

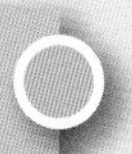

Southern Europe is made up of countries that border with the Mediterranean Sea as well as those farther inland that share a warm Mediterranean climate (see pages 12–13).

Nordic countries 

The Nordic countries include Denmark, Finland, Iceland, Norway, Sweden, and Greenland. Greenland is part of the North American continent, but is also part of the Kingdom of Denmark. It used to be governed by the Danish, and still shares many political and cultural similarities with its former ruler.

Scandinavia 

The countries of Norway, Sweden, and Denmark are known collectively as Scandinavia. They share a common history. In the past, these countries fought each other over their territories, and the people who lived in these countries were known as Vikings.

Baltic states 

The three countries of Latvia, Estonia, and Lithuania are often referred to as "the Baltics." The name comes from the Baltic Sea, with these countries sitting on its eastern coast.

Benelux 

Benelux is a region that unites Belgium, Netherlands, and Luxembourg. These countries established Benelux as a union in 1944. The name is made up of the initial letters of each country: ***Be***lgium, ***Ne***therlands, ***Lux***embourg. They are also referred to as the "Low Countries," as much of their land is flat and below sea level.

Eastern Europe 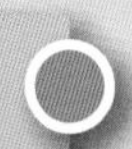

Eastern Europe is made up of Poland, the Czech Republic, Hungary, Romania, Bulgaria, and the countries that are east of these. These countries have histories that connect them to the former Soviet Union (see page 9). Some people include the Baltic States in this region.

Climates

Europe can be divided up into four different **climate** zones: Mediterranean, marine west coast, humid continental, and subarctic. Each zone experiences different temperatures and weather conditions that influence everything from the way people live to the wildlife that are native to the zones.

- Mediterranean
- marine west coast
- humid continental
- subarctic

Subarctic zone

The subarctic climate is cold and snowy with very long winters, and short mild summers lasting from one to three months. The very north of this zone falls into the Arctic Circle, where the ground is permanently frozen, making it difficult for any plants other than mosses and lichens to grow.

Humid continental zone

The climate in Europe's humid continental zone varies between the four seasons, as it does across Europe. But in this zone the differences are felt most strongly.

SPRING	SUMMER	AUTUMN	WINTER
warm and wet	warm and humid	cool and dry	cold and harsh

Marine west coast zone

The marine west coast climate zone is in the path of westerly ocean winds. These winds bring cloudy skies and keep the air over the land cool in summer and mild in the winter.

Mediterranean zone

The Mediterranean climate is known for long, hot, and dry summers and cool, wet winters. The mountain ranges farther inland block out the cold north winds, while hot, steady winds blow in from Africa.

Isotherms

sotherm maps are used to show weather forecasts and an be used to give us an overview of how weather differs cross areas of land. The map on the right shows the verage temperature in January. Each line (isotherm) rosses over an area that has the same temperature.

TEMPERATURE

-0.4 °F (-18 °C)	10.4 °F (-12 °C)	20.3 °F (-6.5 °C)	30.2 °F (-1 °C)	40.1 °F (4.5 °C)	50 °F (10 °C)

Northernmost point

At the northernmost part of Europe is an **archipelago** called Franz Josef Land. It is part of Russia and is made up of 191 islands, which are mainly covered in sheets of ice. Franz Josef Land is an unwelcome place for humans, but a perfect sanctuary for Arctic wildlife such as walruses. It has a record low temperature of –48.1 °F (–44.5 °C).

Southernmost point

A Greek island called Gavdos is located in the southernmost part of Europe. This small island is a popular destination for tourists looking for beaches and hot weather. In the summer, temperatures can reach above 104 °F (40 °C).

SOUTHERNMOST EUROPE

NORTHERNMOST EUROPE

AVERAGE TEMPERATURE

86 °F (30 °C)
77 °F (25 °C)
68 °F (20 °C)
59 °F (15 °C)
50 °F (10 °C)
41 °F (5 °C)
32 °F (0 °C)
23 °F (–5 °C)
14 °F (–10 °C)
5 °F (–15 °C)
–4 °F (–20 °C)
–13 °F (–25 °C)
–22 °F (–30 °C)

JANUARY

JULY

Wettest place

Crkvice, in the mountains of Montenegro, is the wettest inhabited place in Europe. It's within the Mediterranean climate and remains dry during summer, but is rainy the rest of the year. Its average annual rainfall is around 183 inches (464.8 cm), hitting a record 316 inches (803 cm) in 1937.

Driest place

Almería, in southern Spain, is the driest city in Europe. It only experiences around 26 days of rain per year, with an average annual rainfall of just 7.7 inches (19.6 cm).

Wildlife

Europe has a huge range of wildlife, from polar bears in the Arctic to sand snakes in the Mediterranean. Over thousands of years, humans have cut down forests and woodlands, which now cover only about 25 percent of the continent. In some of these forests, you can still see bears and boars, and ancient oak trees.

Peregrine falcon

European elk

Polar bear

Grey seal

Wolverine

European squid

Wild boar

English oak

Tulips

Pine marten

Gallic rooster

Nettle-tree butterfly

Asp viper

Olive tree

Bottlenose dolphin

Atlantic cod

Atlantic cod can be found in the waters around Iceland, Norway, and the United Kingdom (UK). It is one of the world's most popular fish to eat, particularly in the UK, Spain, and Portugal.

Iberian lynx

The Iberian lynx is one of the most **endangered** animal species in Europe, with only around 300 living in the wild. Its habitat in Spain has shrunk because of the construction of roads and growth of towns, and its main diet of rabbit has been reduced by disease.

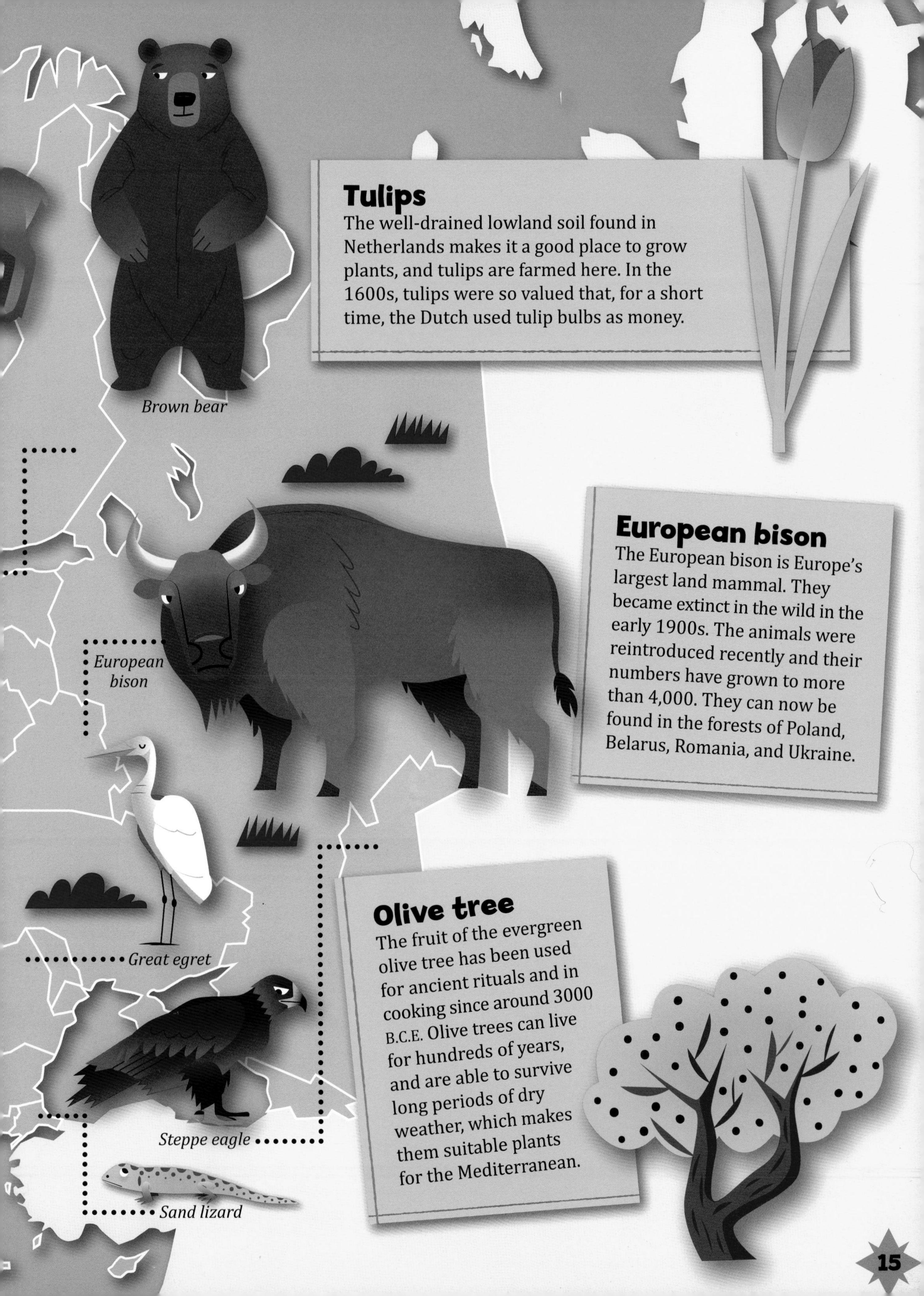

Tulips

The well-drained lowland soil found in Netherlands makes it a good place to grow plants, and tulips are farmed here. In the 1600s, tulips were so valued that, for a short time, the Dutch used tulip bulbs as money.

European bison

The European bison is Europe's largest land mammal. They became extinct in the wild in the early 1900s. The animals were reintroduced recently and their numbers have grown to more than 4,000. They can now be found in the forests of Poland, Belarus, Romania, and Ukraine.

Olive tree

The fruit of the evergreen olive tree has been used for ancient rituals and in cooking since around 3000 B.C.E. Olive trees can live for hundreds of years, and are able to survive long periods of dry weather, which makes them suitable plants for the Mediterranean.

Natural landmarks

Between the ragged western coastlines and the towering mountain border to the east, Europe is dotted and lined with forests and rivers, and an array of natural wonders.

Fjords, Norway

Fjords are long, narrow inlets of water with steep rock walls on both sides. Huge slow-moving **glaciers** carved out the deep fjords. There are more fjords in Norway than anywhere else in the world.

Giant's Causeway

Giant's Causeway in Northern Ireland, UK, is a natural rock formation of around 40,000 interlocking **basalt** columns. Most of the columns are hexagonal, and some are as high as 38.7 feet (11.8 m).

The Irish legend about a giant called Finn McCool tells how he built the causeway to cross over to Scotland to fight another giant. In fact, the causeway was created around 60 million years ago as a result of a volcanic eruption. The **lava** cooled quickly, forming the distinctive hexagonal shapes.

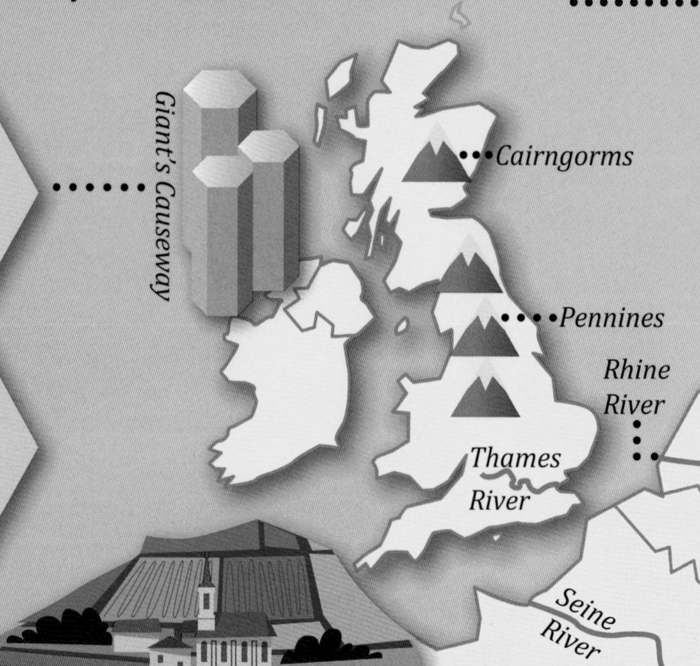

Auvergne Mountains

The Auvergne Mountains are the highest peaks in the Massif Central, an area that is covered with dense forests and extinct volcanoes blanketed in greenery.

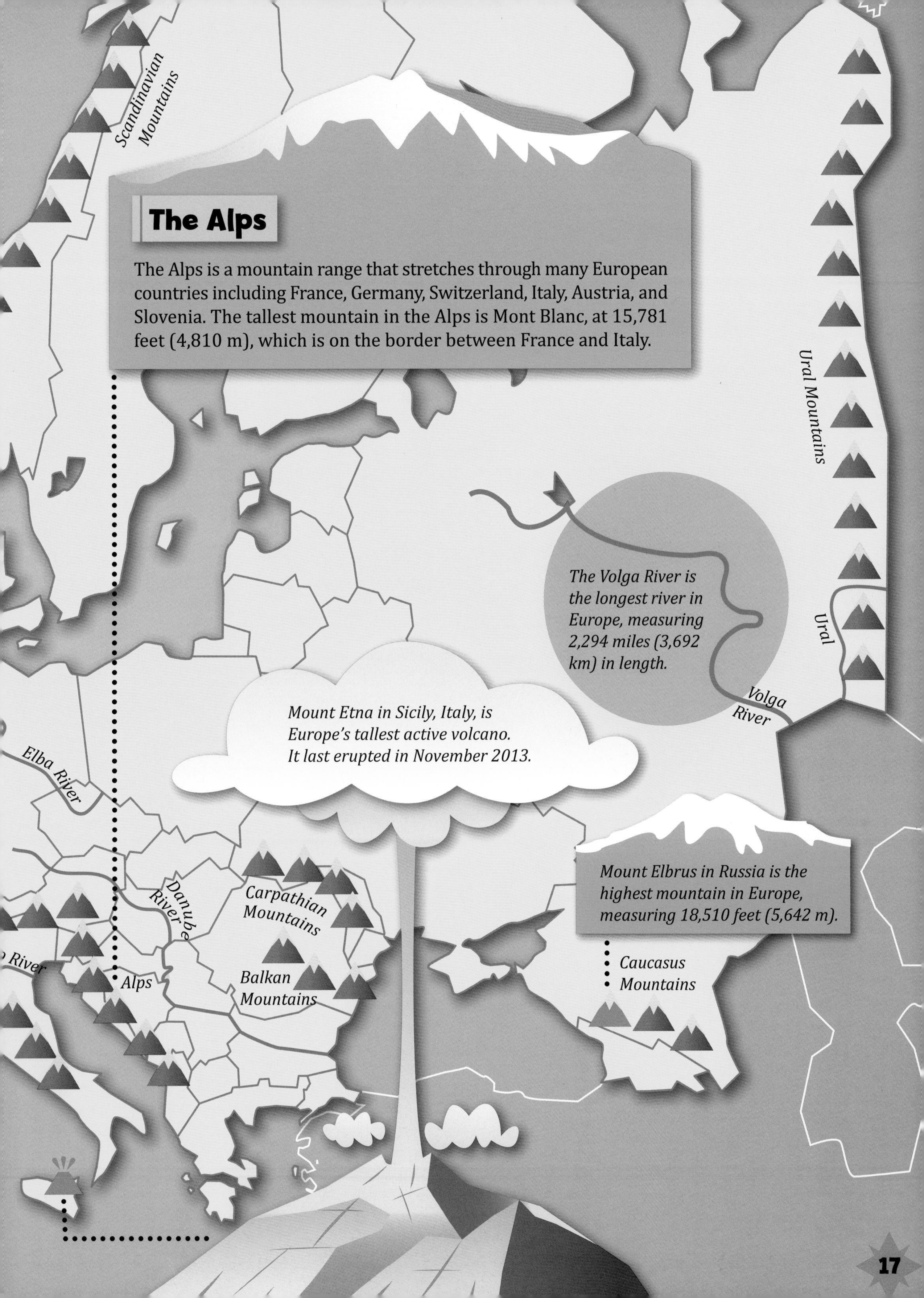

The Alps

The Alps is a mountain range that stretches through many European countries including France, Germany, Switzerland, Italy, Austria, and Slovenia. The tallest mountain in the Alps is Mont Blanc, at 15,781 feet (4,810 m), which is on the border between France and Italy.

Human-made landmarks

From classical columns to giant glass shards, Europe has been a leading force in architecture throughout history. European **architecture** spans thousands of years and many different styles that reflect different histories, cultures, religions, and beliefs.

Caerphilly Castle

There are more than 500 castles in Wales, UK. That's more castles per person than anywhere else in the world. Caerphilly Castle, built in the 1200s, is the largest castle in Wales.

Atomium

The Atomium in Belgium looks like an iron crystal magnified 165 billion times. It was built in 1958 for the Brussels World Fair.

Alhambra

For around 800 years, **Moorish** monarchs (Muslims from North Africa), ruled parts of Spain. They built the fortress and residences of the Alhambra in Granada over a period of several hundred years (800s–1300s A.C.E.) It was later converted into a palace. It contains stunning pieces of Moorish artwork and architecture.

Great Belt Bridge

Measuring 4.2 miles (6.79 km) in length, the Great Belt Bridge is one of the longest bridges in the world. It connects the Danish islands of Funen and Zealand.

Hagia Sophia

The Hagia Sophia, in Istanbul, Turkey, was built between 532 and 537 A.C.E. It was originally a church, then converted into a mosque and is now a museum. It's a space that inspires awe and worship.

Parthenon

The Parthenon, built between 447 and 432 B.C.E., sits atop the Acropolis (high city) in Athens, and stands as a symbol of ancient Greek order and wealth.

Italian architecture

Italy is packed with buildings covering almost 3,000 years of history and many different styles of architecture.

PIRELLI TOWER, 1950s, MILAN

ST MARK'S BASILICA, 832–1094, VENICE

CRESPI'S CASTLE, 1890s, CAPRIATE SAN GERVASIO

LEANING TOWER OF PISA, 1173–1372, PISA

COLOSSEUM

BASILICA OF SAINT MARY OF THE FLOWER, 1296–1436, FLORENCE

POMPEII

NECROPOLIS OF THE BANDITACCIA, 800–200 B.C.E., CERVETERI

VALLEY OF THE TEMPLES, 500s B.C.E., AGRIGENTO, SICILY

Colosseum

The colosseum was the largest **amphitheater** in the Roman Empire. It was built in 80 B.C.E. and could hold around 50,000 spectators. They came to watch gladiators fight each other or fight wild animals.

Pompeii

When the volcano, Mount Vesuvius, erupted in 79 A.C.E. it buried the nearby town of Pompeii under a thick layer of ash. The town was rediscovered in the 1500s and archaeologists have been uncovering the city's remains ever since.

Industries

Europe is a continent with a wide variety of industries, including farming, manufacturing, and tourism. Large networks of pipes and power stations are spread out over the land and in the sea, supplying the energy needed to keep these industries running.

Main industries in Europe

Crops:

Barley

 Fruit

 Corn

 Oats

Rye

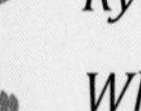 Wheat

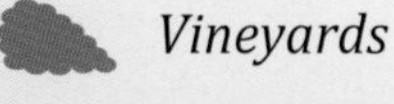 Vineyards

Industries:

 Manufacturing/ industrial areas

 Automobiles

 Forestry

 High tech

 Fishing

Tourism

Livestock:

 Cattle

 Sheep

Pigs

Tourism and France

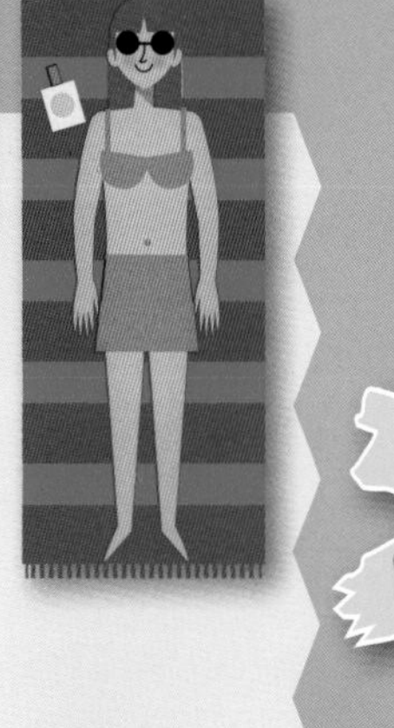

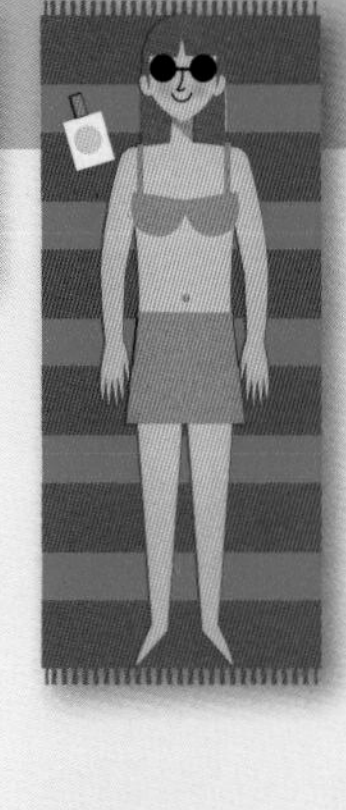

Europe has a long and rich history with hundreds of fascinating tourist sites, but France is the world's most popular tourist destination. More than 10 percent of the population work in tourism.

The number of tourists that visit France each year is bigger than its population! France offers visitors sunny beaches, snowy mountains for skiing, and historical destinations to explore.

Automobiles

The automobile industry is a major employer and contributor of wealth to many countries in Europe, particularly Germany, France, Italy, and the Czech Republic.

The largest producer of cars in Europe is Germany. Around 6 million cars are made in Germany each year and 5 million are produced overseas in German-owned factories. World-famous and popular car brands from Germany include Volkswagen, BMW, Porsche, and Mercedes-Benz.

GERMAN CARS ARE POPULAR ALL AROUND THE WORLD.

Natural resources

We need a supply of energy resources to generate the power that keeps factories manufacturing and farm tractors running, as well as to provide electricity in homes. Different countries in Europe rely on different energy sources. Some have plenty of their own, whereas others have to rely on imports.

Energy:

- OIL
- NATURAL GAS
- HYDROELECTRICITY
- COAL
- NUCLEAR

Natural gas

Natural gas is a **fossil fuel**, created from dead animals and plants buried deep underground that have compressed and decomposed over millions of years. Like other fossil fuels such as coal and oil, we burn natural gas to generate electricity.

Russia has the largest reserve of natural gas and is Europe's biggest supplier of the resource. The gas is delivered through large underground and undersea pipes.

Mapping capital cities

Histories of conflict and trade have shaped many of Europe's capital cities. Many were built around centers of power, such as royal palaces or government buildings. Others were built on the banks of large rives that were important routes for trade and transporting goods.

Moscow

Moscow is the capital of Russia. At the center of this city sits a cluster of towers, historic palaces, and government buildings known as the Kremlin. Kremlin means "fortress inside a city" in Russian. Close by the Kremlin are St Basil's Cathedral and Red Square, where the main streets of Moscow begin.

Paris

Paris, the capital of France, was rebuilt between 1852 and 1870 with wide streets, parks, and squares. This was to allow more space for vehicles to get through, but also to prevent people from forming **barricades** across the streets to protest and to cause disruptions.

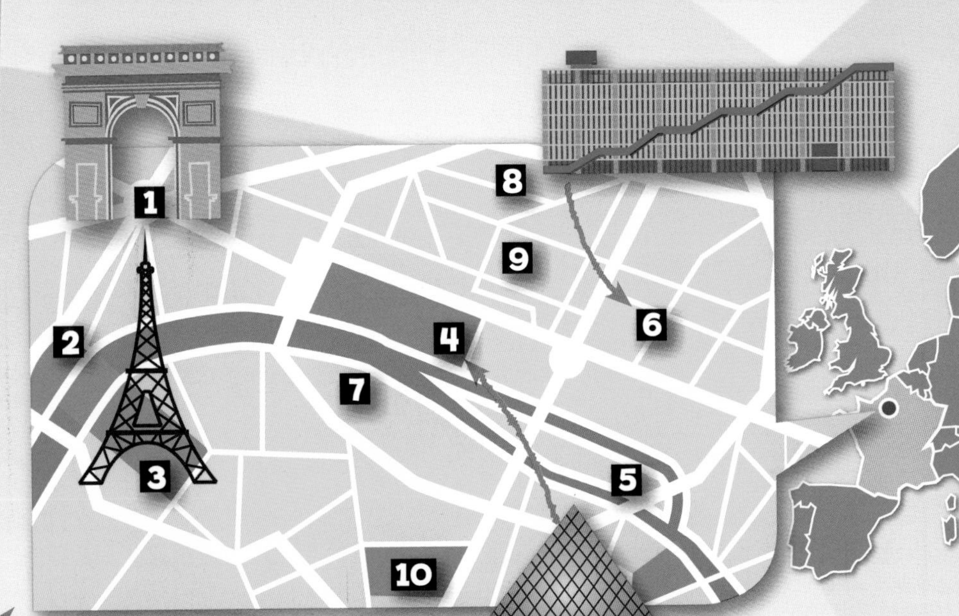

PARIS TOURIST SPOTS:

1 Arc de Triomphe
2 Palais de Chaillot
3 Eiffel Tower
4 Louvre
5 Notre Dame
6 Centre Pompidou
7 Musée d'Orsay
8 Opéra
9 Palais Royal
10 Palais du Luxembourg

Stockholm

Stockholm, the capital of Sweden, is unusual in that it is built around 14 islands. The central island, Stadsholmen—also known as "the old town"—is where the royal palace sits.

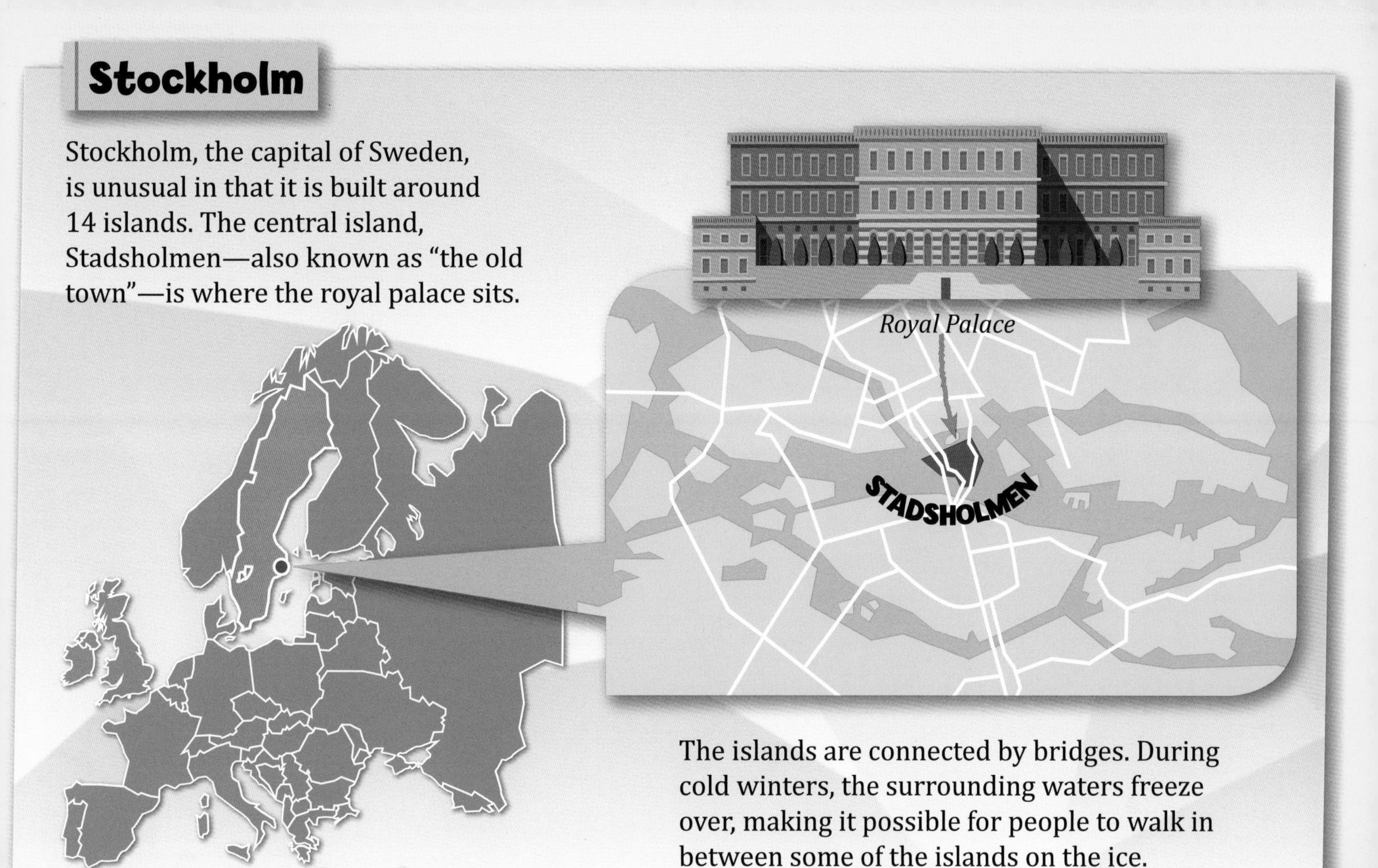

The islands are connected by bridges. During cold winters, the surrounding waters freeze over, making it possible for people to walk in between some of the islands on the ice.

Budapest

Budapest, the capital of Hungary, was two cities: Buda to the west of the River Danube, and Pest to the east of the river.

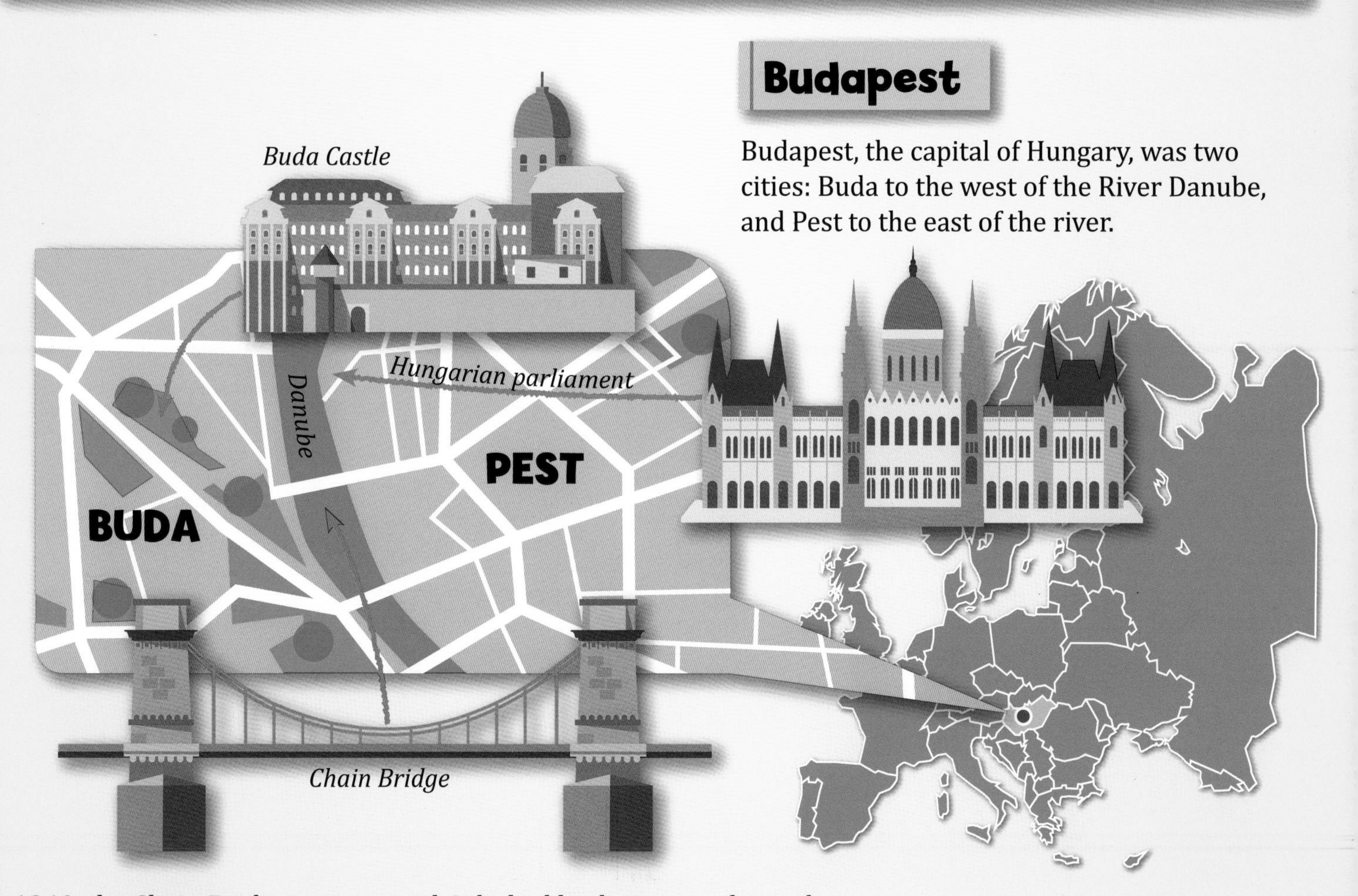

n 1849, the Chain Bridge was opened. It linked both cities and was the irst permanent bridge across the River Danube. However, it wasn't until 1873 that Buda and Pest were officially merged, becoming Budapest.

Sports

Balls, wheels, rackets, and skis are just a few of the items used for sporting tournaments in Europe. Competitions are played at local, national, continental, and international levels.

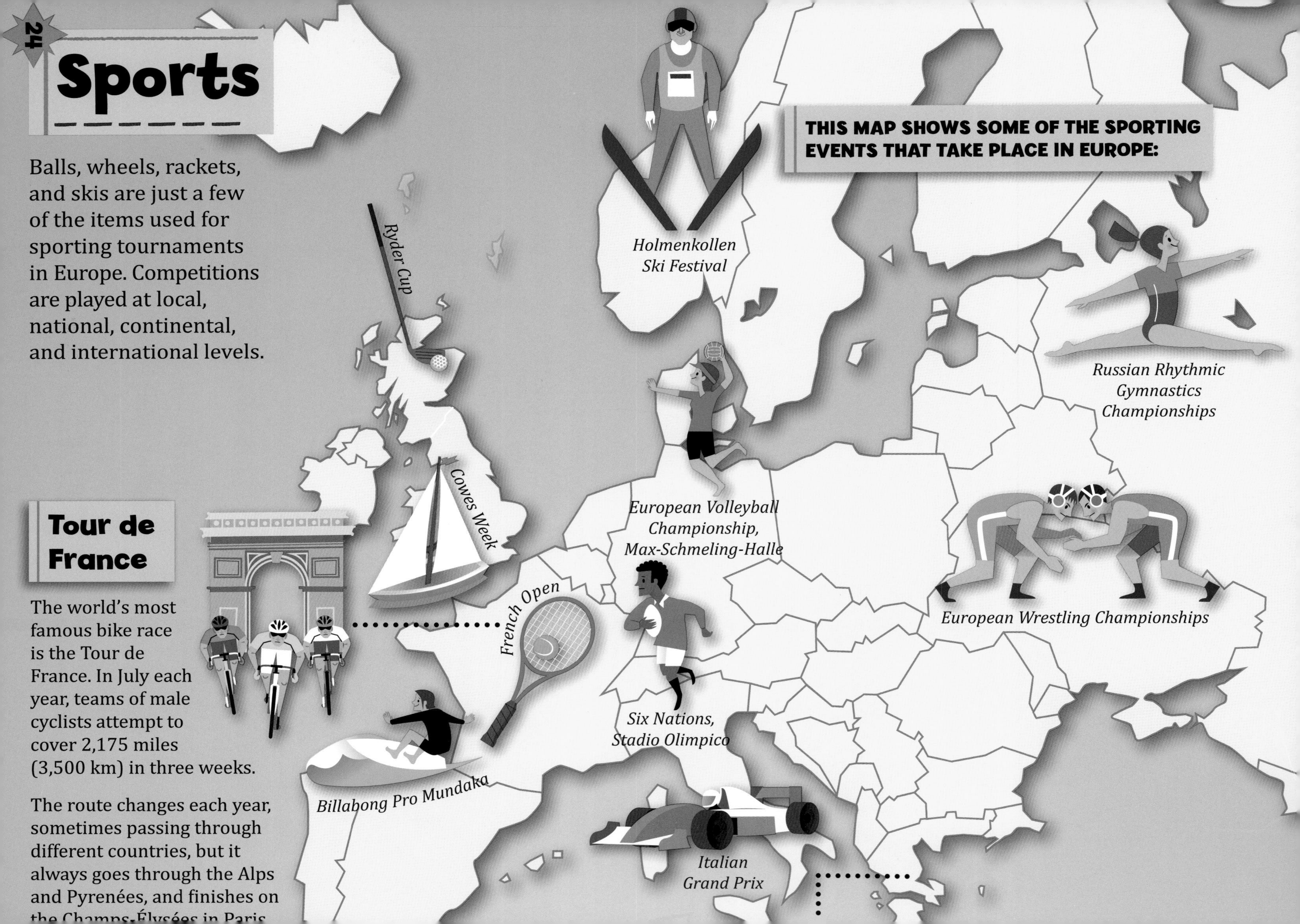

Tour de France

The world's most famous bike race is the Tour de France. In July each year, teams of male cyclists attempt to cover 2,175 miles (3,500 km) in three weeks.

The route changes each year, sometimes passing through different countries, but it always goes through the Alps and Pyrenées, and finishes on the Champs-Élysées in Paris

The Olympic Games

The Olympic Games is the biggest international sporting event in the world. It takes place every four years, with countries from all over the world taking part in more than 90 different competitions.

The first ancient Olympic Games was held in Olympia in Greece in 776 B.C.E., and only Greek men could compete. The ancient Games included running, long jump, javelin, boxing, and chariot races.

The first modern Olympic Games, similar to what we know today, was held in Athens in 1896.

The opening ceremony from the 2012 London Olympic Games.

This ancient Greek vase shows Olympic runners.

Soccer

Soccer, called football in Europe, is by far the most popular sport in Europe. Each country has its own national team that competes in major international tournaments. This includes the UEFA European Championships, which take place every four years in a different European country. Spain and Germany have both won three times—more than any other country.

Past winners of the UEFA European Championships:

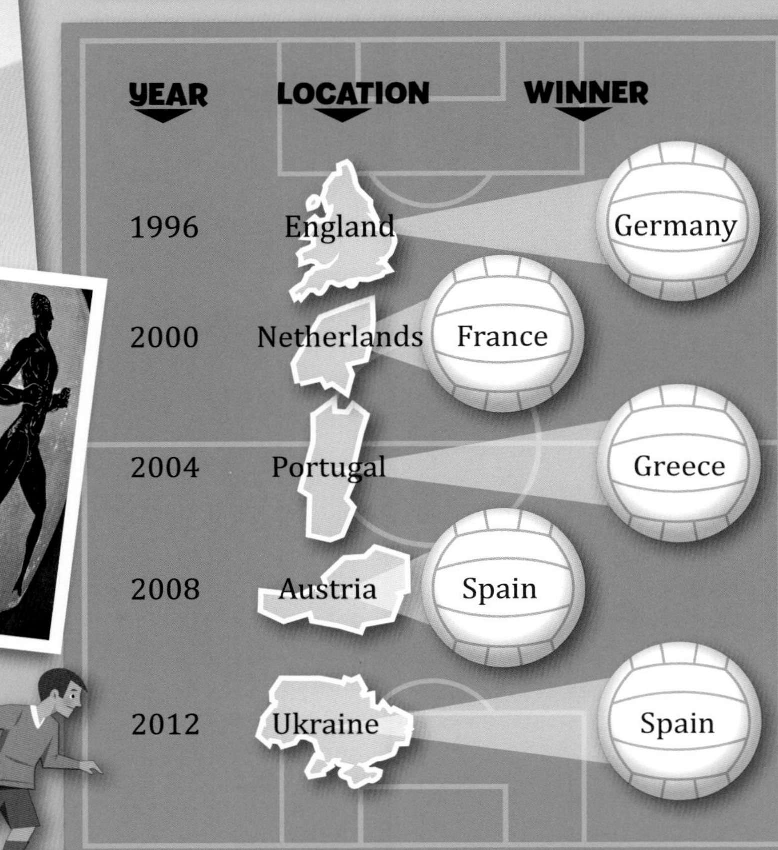

YEAR	LOCATION	WINNER
1996	England	Germany
2000	Netherlands	France
2004	Portugal	Greece
2008	Austria	Spain
2012	Ukraine	Spain

Culture

Europe has blazed a trail in the art world for centuries, producing notable literature, art, music, and dance. Its rich culture has been influenced by religious beliefs, ancient ideas, and developments in technology that have spread out across the continent.

William Shakespeare

William Shakespeare was a poet and playwright, born in Stratford-upon-Avon, England, in 1564. He wrote a total of 37 plays, some of which explore people and moments from history, while others are romances, comedies, and tragedies. His most famous plays include *Romeo and Juliet* and *Hamlet*.

Shakespeare's plays are performed all around the world, with many people considering him to be the greatest writer in the English language.

The Renaissance

The **Renaissance** was a period in European history, from the 1300s to the 1500s, in which artists and scientists explored ideas borrowed from ancient Greece and Rome. The Renaissance brought an explosion of new talent that influenced a change in culture, education, and technology.

The center for Renaissance art was Italy, where artists used new techniques in painting and sculpture to look for different ways to represent the world.

The Mona Lisa *(1503–1517) is a Renaissance painting by Leonardo da Vinci (1452–1519).*

The headquarters of the Catholic Church is Vatican City, a small country inside Rome, the capital of Italy. Vatican City contains the Pope's residence, the Sistine Chapel, and St. Peter's Basilica.

Waltz

The waltz is a dance that was very popular in Vienna, Austria, from the early 1800s, before it spread to the rest of Europe. In the dance, partners hold each other close and glide elegantly around the dance floor.

Austrian composer Johann Strauss wrote a famous waltz called "The Blue Danube," named after the River Danube. The river passes through ten European countries, including Romania, Hungary, Austria, and Germany.

Religion

Christianity is the largest religion in Europe. It has been practiced for more than 2,000 years and is made up of different groups, such as Protestantism, Eastern Orthodoxy, and Catholicism. The Catholic Church has the largest number of followers in Europe. Christianity has had a major influence on how countries have been ruled, and on the arts they have produced.

In the southeastern countries of Albania, Azerbaijan, Kosovo, and Turkey, the majority of the population are Muslims. There, culture is greatly influenced by the religious teachings of Islam.

The Sultan Ahmed Mosque, also known as the Blue Mosque, is in Istanbul, the capital of Turkey. It is filled with chandeliers, wall panels, and stained glass windows with designs inspired by verses from the Quran.

Food and drink

Europe is a continent united by a passion for food and drink. Many countries have their own national dishes, and regions have a strong sense of loyalty to their home-grown cooking and produce.

Parma

Parma ham

Thin slices of dry-cured ham have been produced in Parma for more than 2,000 years. The pigs used to make the ham must be bred in the northern and central regions of Italy. There are currently more than 150 companies in Parma producing Parma ham.

Champagne

Champagne is a type of sparkling wine that can only be made in the Champagne region of France. Other wines may be made in a champagne-like style, but cannot legally be called champagne.

FRANCE

Haggis

A national food of Scotland is the haggis, which is a large sausage made from a sheep's stomach stuffed with chopped sheep's lungs, liver, heart, oatmeal, onion, suet (animal fat), and spices.

Pierogi

A pierogi is a traditional Polish dumpling filled with potato, cheese, and onion. It comes from a region once known as Red Ruthenia, an area that was once part of Poland but today lies in both present-day Poland and Ukraine.

Swiss chocolate

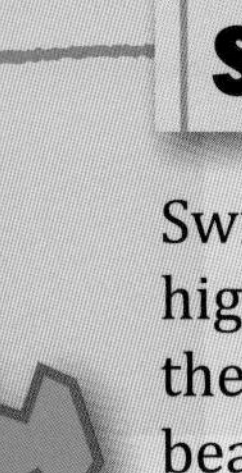

Switzerland is famous for producing high-quality chocolate, even though the main ingredient—the cacao bean—comes from thousands of miles away. It was at a factory in Vevey that milk chocolate was first invented, back in the late 1870s.

Cheese

Cheese is a popular food eaten all over Europe, and there are many different types. Each country, and many regions within these countries, have a type of cheese that is special to the area.

COUNTRY	FAMOUS CHEESE
Italy	Mozzarella di bufala
Britain	Blue Stilton
France	Brie de Melun
Switzerland	Gruyère
Spain	Roncal
Greece	Feta
Netherlands	Edam
Cyprus	Halloumi
Denmark	Danish blue
Norway	Jarlsberg

Further information

COUNTRY	SIZE SQ MI*	POPULATION	CAPITAL CITY	MAIN LANGUAGES
Russia	6,601,665.4 [including Asian territory]	144,031,000 [whole country]	Moscow	Russian
Turkey	302,534.9 [including Asian territory]	81,619,392 [whole country]	Ankara	Turkish
Germany	137,846.9	81,459,000	Berlin	German
France	212,935.3	66,259,012	Paris	French
United Kingdom	94,058.3	65,081,276	London	English
Italy	116,348	61,680,122	Rome	Italian
Spain	195,124.4	47,737,941	Madrid	Spanish
Ukraine	233,031.9	44,291,413	Kiev	Ukrainian
Poland	120,728.3	38,346,279	Warsaw	Polish
Romania	92,043.2	21,729,871	Bucharest	Romanian
Kazakhstan	1,052,089.3 [including Asian territory]	17,948,816 [whole country]	Astana	Kazakh, Russian
Netherlands	16,039.8	16,877,351	Amsterdam	Dutch
Portugal	35,556.1	10,813,834	Lisbon	Portuguese
Greece	50,948.9	10,775,557	Athens	Greek
Czech Republic	30,450.7	10,627,448	Prague	Czech
Belgium	11,786.9	10,449,361	Brussels	Dutch, French, German
Hungary	35,918.3	9,919,128	Budapest	Hungarian
Sweden	173,859.8	9,723,809	Stockholm	Swedish
Azerbaijan	33,436.4 [including Asian territory]	9,686,210 [whole country]	Baku	Azerbaijani
Belarus	80,154.8	9,608,058	Minsk	Belarussian, Russian
Austria	32,382.8	8,223,062	Vienna	German
Switzerland	15,937.1	8,061,516	Bern	French, German, Italian
Serbia	29,912.9	7,209,764	Belgrade	Serbian
Bulgaria	42,810.6	6,924,716	Sofia	Bulgarian
Denmark	16,638.7	5,569,077	Copenhagen	Danish
Slovakia	18,932.5	5,443,583	Bratislava	Slovak
Finland	130,558.5	5,268,799	Helsinki	Finnish, Swedish
Norway	148,186.7	5,147,792	Oslo	Norwegian
Georgia	26,911.3 [including Asian territory]	4,935,880 [whole country]	Tbilisi	Georgian
Ireland	27,132.5	4,832,765	Dublin	Irish, English
Croatia	21,851.1	4,470,534	Zagreb	Croatian
Bosnia and Herzegovina	19,767.3	3,871,643	Sarajevo	Bosnian
Moldova	13,069.9	3,583,288	Chisinau	Romanian
Lithuania	25,212.5	3,505,738	Vilnius	Lithuanian
Albania	11,099.7	3,020,209	Tirana	Albanian
Latvia	24,937.9	2,165,165	Riga	Latvian
Macedonia	9,927.8	2,091,719	Skopje	Macedonian
Slovenia	7,827.4	1,988,292	Ljubljana	Slovene
Kosovo	4,203.5	1,859,203	Pristina	Albanian, Serbian
Estonia	17,462.6	1,257,921	Tallinn	Estonian
Cyprus	3,571.8	1,172,458	Nicosia	Greek, Turkish
Montenegro	5,332.8	650,036	Podgorica	Montenegrin
Luxembourg	998.5	520,672	Luxembourg City	Luxembourgish, French, German
Malta	122	412,655	Valletta	Maltese, English
Iceland	39,768.5	317,351	Reykjavik	Icelandic
Andorra	180.7	85,458	Andorra la Vella	Catalan
Liechtenstein	61.8	37,313	Vaduz	German
San Marino	23.6	32,742	San Marino	Italian
Monaco	0.77	30,508	Monaco	French
Vatican City	0.17	842	Vatican City	Italian

**To arrive at square kilometers (sq km), divide a number in square miles (sq mi) by 0.386102.*

Glossary

amphitheater
an open, circular building with a central space for events, surrounded by an area for spectators

archipelago
a cluster of islands contained within an area of sea

astronomer
a person who studies the stars, planets, and other objects in space

barricades
barriers built across streets to prevent people from passing through

basalt
dark rock formed by volcanic activity

climate
average weather conditions in a particular area

communist
a person, institution, or country that supports communism—a system of ideas and government in which all property is publicly owned and each person is paid according to their needs and abilities

currency
a form of money used in different countries and continents, such as the Euro or the US dollar

democratic
describing or relating to a form of government in which the members of government have been voted in by the country's citizens

endangered
at risk of extinction, or dying out

equator
an imaginary line drawn around the middle of Earth, separating the Northern and Southern Hemispheres

fossil fuel
fuel made from the remains of living things that have been compressed underground for thousands of years (oil, gas, coal)

glacier
a mass of ice that moves very slowly over a large area of land

isotherm
a line on a map that connects areas that have the same temperature

latitude
imaginary lines that run east and west across Earth and are used to help find locations on Earth's surface

lava
hot rock that flows out of a live volcano and cools down to form hard rock

longitude
imaginary lines that run from the North Pole down to the South Pole and are used to help find locations on Earth's surface

Moorish
relating to the people and culture of the North African Muslims that once ruled Spain from 711 A.C.E. to 1492 A.C.E.

Renaissance
describing a period that began in Italy in the early 1400s, where artists, scientists, and philosophers studied ancient Roman and Greek culture to find new ways to represent and explore the world

transcontinental
something that crosses over into more than one continent, such as the borders of a country or a railway line

Index